Rollercoaster Fun!

Written by Jillian Powell
Illustrated by Stefania Colnaghi

WAYLAND

Rosie went for a
rollercoaster ride.

Megan went too.

"I love rollercoasters!"
Rosie said.

"Me too!" Dad said.

Rosie sat with Megan.

"Look, Megan!" she said.
"We're off!"

"Oh no!" Megan said.

"Here we go!" Dad said.
"Wave to Mum!"

The rollercoaster went up.
"Hurray!" Rosie said.

"Oh no!" Megan said.

The rollercoaster stopped. "Hold on!" Dad said.

Whoosh! The rollercoaster
went down.

"STOP!" Rosie shouted.

They went faster
and faster.

"Hurray!" Megan shouted.

They screamed as they
went up.

They screamed as they
went down.

Then the rollercoaster
stopped.

"Time to get off,"
Dad said.

"Let's go again!"
Megan said.

"No thank you! I feel sick!"
Rosie said.

START READING is a series of highly enjoyable books for beginner readers. They have been carefully graded to match the Book Bands widely used in schools. This enables readers to be sure they choose books that match their own reading ability.

The Bands are:

| Pink / Band 1 |
| Red / Band 2 |
| Yellow / Band 3 |
| Blue / Band 4 |
| Green / Band 5 |
| Orange / Band 6 |
| Turquoise / Band 7 |
| Purple / Band 8 |
| Gold / Band 9 |

START READING books can be read independently or shared with an adult. They promote the enjoyment of reading through satisfying stories supported by fun illustrations.

Jillian Powell started writing stories when she was four years old. She has written many books for children, including stories about cats, dogs, scarecrows and ghosts.

Stefania Colnaghi lives with her husband in a small village near Pavia, in northern Italy. She loves drawing animals and naughty children and in her free time enjoys walking in the hills around her home with her dogs.

Rollercoaster Fun!

First published in 2008
by Wayland

Text copyright © Jillian Powell 2008
Illustration copyright © Stefania Colnaghi 2008

Wayland
338 Euston Road
London NW1 3BH

Wayland Australia
Hachette Children's Books
Level 17/207 Kent Street
Sydney, NSW 2000

Series Editor: Louise John
Editor: Katie Powell
Cover design: Paul Cherrill
Design: D.R.ink
Consultant: Shirley Bickler

A CIP catalogue record for this book is available from the British Library.

ISBN 9780750252225

Printed in China

Wayland is a division of Hachette Children's Books,
an Hachette Livre UK Company
www.hachettelivre.co.uk